Samhain

by

Russell Buker

Copyright © *Samhain* by Russell Buker

All rights reserved. No part of this book may be reproduced without the express permission of the author, except in the case of brief excerpts embodied in critical articles and reviews.

Published by Piscataqua Press
an imprint of RiverRun Bookstore
32 Daniel Street
Portsmouth NH 03801

ISBN: 978-1-944393-92-2

Contents

The Handwriting is	1
Sow-in	2
Markings in pain	4
At night	5
Weather	7
Abrogated	8
Emergency Prayer	10
Nearer	12
Tashlich	14
That's funny	16
Rent	18
Mother's fog	20
Wanderer	22
There is	24
Attentive	26
A walk in the park	28
It is not	30
Fall's	32
Then that's it	34
Waldeinsomkeit	36
Earth shine	38
Secret	39
Nov 15 2016	41
Pillow talk	43
Full cold moon	45
Winter solstice 2016	46

Document	48
Adaptive optics	49
Full Moon Friday 13th	51
Mutability	53
Dry	54
Dead of winter	56
In the night	58
Spring	59
Secret friend	61
Ditch witch	63
Often	65
Eunoia	66
On	67
Instance and evidence	69
Reality	71
Stars	72
Me	73
Sprung	75
Electron spinning	77
Moving on	79
Limited and intuitive	81
Stuck	82
Chat Bot	83
Disturbed bliss	85
Obsequious emphases	86
Boundaries of being	87
Sure	89
Fend for yourself	91

Perhaps	93
Benevolence	95
Found	96
Leela	97
Balance	100
Words	101
Head tide	102
Gravity wins	103
Sic transit	105
Zhu Xi's reading	107
I remain bearish	109
Inundated	110
This room	111
Sunrise, sunset	113

Add-ons

By my Faith	117
Home	118
Sancutuary	119
Imagine	120
Another day recuperating	122
Ginger	124
Take the A	125
Beaver Moon	126
On the line	128
Night voyage	130
Flume	132
Fear not	133

Time slot	135
Inclinations	137
Early December	139
To you kind sir	140
Hypnagogia	144
Solar stone	146
ah	148
New Year's Day	149

Samhain

The handwriting is

Away from everything
especially me:
bar
die

no, cry it's against
my
f sharp minor
signature,

inertia,
boredom,

arrogance to the
blade edges
of gravity's bent
time

for
me,
exhausted and breathless,

I glide
jump
anonymously
knees
flexed

for once life
remains
speechless

Sow-in

Here heart begins with
h
the race is on attempting
proof
especially when the proof's
100
and we stall, uneasy, soaring
sky-
ward in towering spruce
sparks

Celtic legend tells us that in the
three
feet between heaven and hell
that
somewhere in the midst there
appears
a small crack where ancestors
can
reappear as they have been
thinned,
living and not, living beyond
their
years here and patiently waiting

when they re-arrive they can
become
angered, no one recognizes
them
nor do they recognize any
one
as we have changed so much

in
a single year as we begin to
resemble
features of themselves, un-
recognizable
now to what they were before their
spool
ran out and we rejoice not being
rendered
lately in their secret world
drawn
to us by our precious flame

Markings in pain

love's called our pain
prescribed map's
attempt to regain
whirling lineage's
youthful thrust again

by opening bottles
for each other:
hands still warm,
down on one knee
denouement, denouement

yet it is also plain
our wish to remain
among those musts
grateful trusts
unhurt, well fed

oh my storgay
where would you
like your shot today

At night

ghosts at night
used
to announce
with
galloping hooves

now all I hear is
fluttering
of bat wings
soft

whir as they
pass
by me slowly
from
room to room

I admired those
hooves
of feel and that
whir-
darkened pearls
yet
always knew I
wrote
furiously when
thinking

I might die
any-
time soon as
this
is later again

Weather

there is no sun today
yet
birds are flying to
feeders,
weathering cat stalks
the
underbrush, then why
am I
so content to remain
inside

well there is no rescuing
me
nor any escape in spite
of
linen fog's gentle folds
through
a dissonance this difficult
in
any reconciliation: what-
ever

I was in my past is
now
embedded with acquired
help-
lessness and resists those
remaining
leaves lantern promises
for
help along the way

Abrogated

voiceless leaves
break
from trees without
spring's
fanfare

gasping their true
colors-
Lincoln's red letter
Oking

the hanging after e-
mancipating
slaves- of 38 starving
Dakotas

who had the audacity
to abrogate
their gated, starving
treaty

so it seems because
nothing
has changed in our
super
civilized

twenty first century that
our
politicos still lie & promise
& cheat

us in the largest sham
hanging
in this countries
history

Emergency prayer

there is a filmy,
humid
Southern wind en-
gagging
land today reminiscent
when
digestive fluids crept

silently
without any light
guidance
from a split vessel,
found
attraction and I wondered
what
I was to become in this
bowl

of awful and so one
day
did not feel that
I
was brave enough to
feed
the birds when this

may
be my last day, no
longer
a drawn line, what
we
thought was lost in
primeval

atoms at low energy
radiation
and proton-less my
life
assumed a bowl
floating
dark,

blue waters of the
quiet
universe wondering
am I
attracting or repelling
clicking
on other bowls I could

not
see into as we clicked
away
from one another in the
vain
hope no one would rile
these
waters

Nearer

there was no wind
today,
saturated stillness,
felt sense,
more or less all
that I
have been gnaw-
ing
birth rings from

buffering, buffering
you're
no cleaner than
that
hyena that has your
throat
so how does it feel
waking
to regret at the end

our dream of at least
not
nothing beyond the
mechanical
chewing of of time,
ours,
till the end of time
that
flew from me to me

my course how swiftly
it
flew as masked anxiety
succumbing
to being out of touch
yet
I will never regard
you
as anything but moon-

light
rippling through me
until
I could not stand the
pre-
dawn buffering ache.
of
what I was told about
nonsense

Tashlich

bread on the leaves
for
everyone who loves
as
I do and has a story
to tell
of the beautiful beech-
wood
that flanked the entrance
to my
fields or the surprise
change
of light encountered
crossing
one street to another
oh
flanerie watching my
reflection
storefronts proving myself
again,
again glistening with
another
part of my past perhaps
making
me uneasy hastening
footsteps
or causing pause as
when
gathering an apple
before
entering the expanse
of

a 40 acre field till I
can
not walk without the
sharp
mechanical thudding
having
to get somewhere

That's funny

today was your still
New
England fall day- light
with
a wave length too long
for
our eyes, knife thin,
open
so that my landscape
receded

having outlived all
my
plans, successful or
not,
now I don't have to
wait
till I forget as I sat by
my
window idly noticing
wind

I picked up a book of
mine
written by my mind
started,
gently at first, carving
with
a pen like Exacto knife:
recognizing
a favorite swimming
hole,

a college library seat
where
my reading imagination
could
soar into the intake
vent
of the air handling unit
how
strange any life remaining
now
depends on my carving

Rent

If this kills me
you're
driving home

green
screened she's invisible
except

arms and face and
wolves
know this camera

is
still on them
worse

eagles come anyway
spite
of supposed ghosts

who
supposedly speak
to

me in twilight or
just
before the sun screened

Venus
makes her comeback- oh yes
it's

a heated conversation:
they
try to get me to

believe
that when we all die
we

do not go up into the
stars
rather it's a long, long

drop
into another galaxy
where
we must convince the
living
that there is no such

thing
ascending heavenward to
drop

Mother's fog

beautiful fog mists
on
an alzheimer tundra
oh
what wont we want
to
forget or are encouraged
to

will I remember
her
sitting imobile, gazing
full
ahead not looking at
family
remembering our own
youth's

or gaze beyond all of
unsayables,
defamiliarizations
as
an old Innu who knows
time
and how to occupy ones-
elf

in senility and begins
her
love us back after her

son
sets her in the right
direction
gazing beyond compre-
hension's

universal consciousness
to best
occupy dementia's acute
lone-
liness, bearing fears of
non-
recognition as no one
watches

the quiet devastation
sitting
on the ice, humming to
her-
self and the creeping
cold,
creeping white, hungry
bears

Wanderer

It is not

as though I wanted to
write

them as salvation
yet

in fact when I
decided

to leave I was, as
usual,

solitary and you were
nowhere

in sight while things
disappeared

from my eyes and
mind's

convolutions yet I still
cling

to the lake's banken
hoping

to stay hydrated this
warm,

droughtful year as the
lake

and I try to remain
placid

in recession's low water
march

There is

no lack of providence
no

but where have we
heard

stars shining
How long
I hovered bird-
like

in such a reworked
linguistic

tight pattern

how I wish to
forget

songs that came
from

dying Pelicans

forget swallowed gusts
of wind

as I was unused to
air

that thick or the copied

moon-
light brightening barnacles

who
have just returned

from

the bottom on whale
noses

now resting on stones
as

purposedly placed

recognizing
that I know nothing

of
these going on's

so

far

down that even whales
need

something to tell
them

this is deep enough

Attentive

I had begun to hate
the veneer
I had become, yet
it seemed way too
late to change

that summer was
air-
conditioner hot,
humid
so I mostly sat on

the beach
through the night
drawing
on the hard sand
between

tides and especially
remember
that was the summer
she
promised to sleep with

me
through the agitated
noise
of water's loose sand-
song

I did ask again but
lost
my version in the roar
as
her heels and elbows

familiarized
themselves on the words
drawn
deeper and deeper on the
strand

A walk in the Park

*or how little right any
of
us has to be whoever
we are*

I need hope for another
day
in a large city to
get
that image of her
eyes
off me. Perhaps some
deli
and then a walk on a
side-
walk where no one
catches
my eyes like that
old
sow who was hiding
her
young from me without
a word,
noise as she stared at
me

motionless and I knew
better
than to engage her
then
either her eyes or mind
as

we were on such different
paths
only I was slow backing
un-
obtrusively looking in
all
the nearby trees hoping
not
to see a cub at all as
that
may very well have
prompted
defensive action on her
part

without a changing corner
light
as I crossed looking for a
pharmacy
for this headache that
had
prompted this stumbling
trail
walk in the first place

It is not

as though I wanted to
write

them as salvation
yet

in fact when I
decided

to leave I was, as
usual,

solitary and you were
nowhere

in sight while things
disappeared

from my eyes and
mind's

convolutions yet I still
cling

to the lake's banken
hoping

to stay hydrated this
warm,

droughtful year as the
lake

and I try to remain
placid

in recession's low water
march

Fall's

reason enough
to keep a nut-
hatcher's balance,
singularity,
for a weapon
that I use
constantly:

clean edges
kept sharp and
not being
mathematical
realize Black
Hole's center's
center tears

everything :
how quickly
I would crumble
in spite of
ultimate gravity
held as my
many parts

zoomed away
painfully
screaming that's
the price one
pays not gathering,
storing thoughts
enough

and the price
one pays
for limiting
access to be
remembered
as words
whittled away

Then that's it

all
had happened was

on
that dreary morning

See ya
was all I could

think
to say to our

pesky
red squirrel's

flying
trip in an owls

talon
All I could think

to say
that soggy morning

feels
so stupid, numb

or
selfish as I did

not
want to imagine

those
gleeful, anticipatory

eyes
as mother approached

her
soft-down nest

and
Red's purgatory

Waldeinsamkeit
feeling of being alone in the woods

whistle, warble, click
and
screech, grackles are
practicing

I need a light turning
as
I always seem to be
stepping

on my secretive
shadow
whenever sunshine
splashes

near enough to the
under-
story of tall oak
trees

and songs of war
grackles
perfected over the
years

listening to shrubs,
small
trees or ferns fighting
for

their share of flame
fame
while I stand too still
remembering

bits of Mozart
rolling
through acrid fog
between

the flashes reflected
off
the backs of dead
birds

in
murmuration's
holiest
stall and so I really need
a move

the leaves agree

Earth shine

Now is
the time

shifting prayers
when

dreams I have
imagined

are not enough
ever

moon looming
Neander finds

himself in thal,
his wife,

they both hear a
low vowel growl,

his, of self diss,
dissatisfaction

with himself
fearing this large

moon that seems
to want to tell

someone some-
thing: her or him

Secret

weeds are taking
over

how does one
mourn

for this lake
I

have never seen
water

this low in all
the years

lived here: I
know

they are temporary
beings

but my energy
seems

lower and sit
stewing

in my cosmic
juices

friends do not
call

or write and wonder
how

long before the
veneer,

with all due
respect,

I've built over
years

of gentrifying
will

take to boil
away

a heart that softens
pumping

oxygen
to these gasping

fish

November 15, 2016

Even in these bleak November days
there's gladness for the heart that heeds
Charles Dawson Shanly

How sad
watching my cat
lose all
nine lives, tuneless
number,

while sleeping in
discomfort,
not eating and
once in
a while a small

cry that
stalls in my day-
light's
loss to bring an
evolution

of the dark where
Demeter
sleeps her poppy-seed
dreams
while Persephone's

unkind sun:
scentless, disintegrating
backs
itself below her
horizon

sleep for everyone
settles
below supple moon
flows
silently counting,
counting

Pillow talk

Wait a minute
wait
how implausible
this
Archimedes platform
seems
seems now- just a
minute-
we
really liked her

yet
she disappeared into
a cider
of silence as your
talking
grew on me and my
realities
changed, for better
or worse, and
your omniscient

chatter
lately interrupted
by
the fires of sleep,
in turn
interrupted with
nightly
pains burning up
through
hollow legs to a

fearful
shoulder blade phone
call
in the darkness- how
many
years, miles away
and
now you have gone
want to keep you
forever

silent
as though you knew,

all
along, this would
happen
till we have nowhere
to go
before my knowing
who,
whom we were

and
why we copied
your
realities
of choice, fears and
wordiness
no memories,of illusory
time
left or

Full Cold Moon

every step taken
was
one away from songs

invisible
on a journey home
were

you able to see the
glorious
ring around the

moon-
the I with a white
noose

dizzy with all
this
perspective

now
wonder will I ever be
home

for I'm still hungry
though
I've eaten so much

Winter solstice 2016

I have already
dipped
my toast in
coffee

hurrying to finish
on
this the shortest
day

as if we are starting
again
every day buoyant
atoms

in a glass goblet
seeking
energy, excitation
afraid

of the whorl, hum
within
ready to flour my-
self

urge my self towards
loaf,
loafing, rising: flush
words

among the long shadows
soon
hidden in the darkest
night

where my patience can
best
be described as atoms
do

to their glowing goblet:
disorder
worse when feet interfere
walking

Document

limber, green Pine's
branches
and wind printing

all
the vowels on a
blue

sky and shredded
clouds
trailing consonants

we
are no longer alone
risen

Adaptive optics

blue before dawn
standing
between fir trees
that
include

as I toss old
bread
onto the crystals
for
skittish Ravens

I
take care not to
buttress:
buttress myself against
usual

banked slip slides
wondering
where is our sugar
from
living trees keeping

stumps
alive for memory's
sake
composting under moss
for

all our sake's and
stone-
less reverence as I
touch
the warm tree prior

to
leaving for the house
and
not miss anything in this
Dawn's
latent life flare

Full Moon Friday 13th

Here, more gloom,
the pigs
are butchered, dead

eyes
ache staring at
screens:

computers, front door
drizzling
with dew, streaks in

our
maples, and yes,
darkness

extends to where we
kept
our shoats in sun

-

today is a good day
to bury
what's left out,

needs
to go, gone to the
dark,

unseen words, breath-
less,
where sun waits

for
their declarer behind
doors,

curtains, to give them
their
names back, shaven,

immaculate
from
stiff freezer wrappings

Mutability

upstairs or in my
attic

clouds were ripping
what

screams were left in
trees

now that most leaves
are

gone and every rustle's
intended

I have offered self
way

too long, thin blooded,
arthritic

still proffer perceptions.
Hate

if everyone so loved
blindly

yet still will supplicate
as

there is nothing left:
sun-

sets glow and agony
of sleep

Dry

this is getting nerve-
wracking

I am the Palliser Tri-
angle

words sit empty, dry
clay

containers: dry even
underneath

rising sun, still no
rain

wake my wife to watch
lone

figure who walks every
good

day on the beach's
thinnest

water head bent, slow
steps

knowing this was return
embarking

as we are written, still
tidal,

by our steady intention's
large

rocks that contains her,
her

fluid sand's stars reachable
waiting

to be touched with human
intention

Dead of Winter

To my wife of a
thousand years

keep breathing
in a bag of water

and a tremendous noise
roar breaks from her middle

more words swell, we
sobbed lake's natural end

where we have floated
stubbornly caffeinated

on a shrinking pond's
mycorrhiza's low level

processing to which
I have no access, no

ability to experience
like the rasping sugars

in my kidneys always
excreting excess as I

welcoming doline,
polynya's cantilevers

slow failure and in our
adaptations during excess

of water or drought changing
evergreen to deciduous

stripping dripping leaves
faultless in changing seasons

and we fought off falling
asleep as stalagmites

treacherous gaze, child-
like, kept growing, un-

noticed, steadily, drip

by drip by drip-
a geography of waves

In the night

pardon me
if

the light shining
be

tween us
looked tensile

and you
fell

then I
fell

couldn't we
have

waited for
day light

Spring

if no one will pitch,
contest
of wills-one of three,
best
to look for fastball
high-

to Babe Ruth in heaven
when
the outfield's shower
of
indignation's so short

and
what of the ball's space-
travel
courtesy of bat's recoil held
loosely
in Bambino hands

presume
that he hands the bat to
Ironman
and we have a game
with
red threads spinning way

out
in the universe beyond
crack
of a named ashen slug
tell
them how we fought

for
long strikes that we now
dump
back onto the field as if
we
know how to say good by

Secret friends

Have a look, secret friend,
distant one:
I'm the icy and sad
light of dawn...
and as icy and sad,
morning come,
I shall die, distant friend,
and be gone.
         Ossip Mandelstham

I could almost
despair, yet,
feel a certain
freedom
to write whatever
enters
my thoughts and now
feel the urge

to hurry
as someone has
just
told me that we,
sapiens,
will be extinct in
less
than a century

my mother or
father did not have
to
imagine this and
hurried
a family of four
along
shafts of light we chose

and then they left:
no
talks over cups of
coffee
as I regaled them
anecdotal

of the stubborn man,
they
had raised, attempts
at
filleting my heart
onto
pages while saner
people

dug away at the
earth
before Africa split
into
three more parts
surrounded
by swiftly moving
Red

Seas dust on a surprised
beach
as a sun rose, hesitant, to
zenith
slowly rolling to darkness

Ditch Witch

I caught glimpses of
you
in the arroyo three days
before
the next bad storm

for you it is a
matter
of self confidence:
dark
matter cresting higher

dark matter among eager
cries
of trapped children tricked:
you
tricked with trinkets

in soft, dry sand
see
you hovering among
shiny
dreams you dropped

now you stand on jammed
debris,
La Llorona, sifting in
moving
sticks to claim another

dead child before the
waters
stop and everyone
will
be looking for you

Often

Mornings
I often wonder:
does
one have to die

to
allow their soul
wings
of waxen feathers

freedom
in looming morning's
steep
price in becoming

light
while handling the
wheel
as my lobster boat

my sleepy lobster boat
clears
the harbor floating
on

gentle tugs underneath
resur-
ected surf from the open
sea

Eunoia

Greek
for beautiful thinking

Just when I
needed

thought my writing
had changed

into a washer ball
after drifting

along like a soul
unsure if

it is aging or just
waiting

1 and 2- drummers go
stick-crazy

with dark-coated monks
spattering blessings

no holy wars
for them

oh no, they come at
night time

pilfering my anecdotes
working

through basic incomes,
inequality

On

sorrows thin
chest

worse when
words

when melting
snow

dragged haggling
voices

reflecting in the
still-

life jumbo
word-

find, found curled in
womb,

that's marshaled
here

where every
one

waits for
wind:

anything and
every-

thing until
propaganda's

talus
slide slams

in the lake,
dust

floating dims
aging

languages sonic
sound

Instance and evidence

though unseen this
moon
is waxing, morning
stars:
Mercury, Venus, Mars,
Uranus,
and Neptune are not
visible
and I am back to my
youth

Mysterious shapes,
tethered,
the shore is full of
boats,
tenders, I would like
my
courage back and take
next
row out into the
harbor,

see the boats from mid
current
while they seem so
sleepy
one wonders if they
will
ever jaunt out to
moored
ladies before we tourists
this

placid water and choose
my
dream of instance and
evidence
or fog will drift away
leaving
me still alone, likely
older

Reality

what are you
doing?
just
re calibrating
with
reliable lantern,
sun
exciting glass

tried
to tell her that
one
does not recover
from
a coma as we
only
get mind, body,

soul,
flares of sun
allowed
and a person has
three
short seconds to
answer
before wheeled

home
in anger, muzzled
already
in another reply

Stars

today is May
tenth
the moon is full
morning
stars are Mercury, Venus,
Mars,
Uranus and Neptune
it has been like
that
for a few days
now
also, when I was
young
I loved to watch
those
stars shine on
me

think how lovely
to have
many more
mother's
to help me
untangle
thought from non-
human
words that define
my
turgidity, so many
more
to memorize, learn
before
mother called for
breakfast

Me

I see you on the dock
that
always floats away
every
spring, moving with
slow
tides and harsh winds

I see you packed
in
different boxes,
drawers
in the quiet attic
where
some poems lie
scattered

who has been re-
reading
these written so
long
ago and now they,
turning
yellow decorating one
half

of a picture of you in
sepia
the other half in black and
white
but where is the color
shared
in the autumn of pure
agitation,

silent breathing's of a
twin
soul separating itself
one
black and one white
belonging
to
neither, freeing the dock

Sprung

She said
how similar it
is
awakening from
dream
that wont let
go

patient,plodding
green
skin, set backs
growing
over whatever
winter
did

lying on turned
soil
to recover from
from
thrust of green
through
the laconic smile

of sleeping winter:
also,
dressing you doll-
like
with all your Meds
swallowed
with driving rain

hoping
you'll outlive me,
nor
will I be blamed
for
these wind- tattered
clothes

Electron spinning

*New experiment
confirms
that reality does
not
exist if you are
not
looking at it
or reality does not
exist
until it is measured
at
least on the atomic
scale*

I am now thinking
apples,
oranges whizzing
about
my head as I step
onto
the deck in pre-
dawn
to feed the birds,

wonder
if they still exist
as
they did yesterday
because
I can not see them
nestled
on a branch, in a
nest

unseen and unmeasured
How
exciting that none of
us
exist in the coming
light
as protons frantically
spin
looking for my memories
shape

Moving on

Full frontal, glamorous
clouds

this is dangerous
for
until the winds
start
up again and moving
clouds:
their
limp bodies spilled,
looking
dumb throat-ed, but
have
finally
been able to see
their
soft undersides with
cool,
dark lake-glass reflection,
and
their
known excuses help-
lessly
ingesting mad grackles
with
all that flapping,
cawing
noise
as they tracked through
summer
just as many relatives
moved

from
place to reinvented
place
but now call a place
they've
never
lived their home with-
out
noticing
that the wind has started.
moving
their clouds again

Limited and intuitive

taint of the silent page
where
everything begins as a
lie
keeping every word
imbued,
those daubs, ink-dark
bread
crumbs, on a still water
where
shade trees learn to
grow
up and out, people too
who
quickly become lost as
families
in a dark forest and they
call
to me at noontime or
when
moonshine covers their
world
as they know it and fear
swimming
in flowing liquids, bumping
into
things that can not be good
for
their strewn, lido souls
desiring
to turn this page for more
exciting
things like bullets, bombs
and
dead babies; stuff that they
know

Stuck

To me it is like
fence-
walking during
first
love mad to cap con-
templating
whether I'm real or
just
dreaming especially
now
that I am this super
age
with strange dreams
nightly

stuck
dangling in those
mandibles
of time as we know
it
unfeeling feet source-less
listening
for the crackling crunch
like
the ring-tone timer
that
has rung way too
long

Chat Bot

homesick now I
can
really imagine a
world
without me as
simul-
taneous internal
existence
less my glorious
suit
worn by my true
self
now a blur in an
undected
molecule methyl
oso-
cyanate light years
away
created in the seed
Chat
Bot borrowed from
me
in lines of well
rooted
grass settling in the
drought
I shared with beautiful
women
who bore the sharpest
tongues

songs that frightened
me
knowing I had willingly
passed
my mind to software

Disturbed bliss

How bright of you
silent waxing
buoyed
without a beginning

on a yearly basis
strawberry moon
low in my sky
yet so far away

and love's cooling
task wanes to a
sliver of hope
fruit will wax

Obsequious emphases

I have decided to
store
tattered old poems in
form-
aldehyde blameless
tortured
words that have only
one
meaning-multitude
words
one meaning that can be
seen
from any angle by
turning
the silent, odious jar
around
that reeks of Poetry's
one
meaning that calmly drew
befuddled
Jack to the hilltop for a better
view
with Jill in a downpour of
rain

Boundaries of being

I remember dad as
we
watched you dig a
hole
in our garden by the
wall
that kept us from our
neighbor's
lawn

seemed to take you
forever
but at last you picked
up
the bag filled with
notes
to Crazy our cat for
so
immortal long

placed it gently and
started
filling in the hole
Crazy
I remember the day
dad
brought you home
in
a cloth bag set between

and
the noise you made
escaping
now wishing to make
that
same noise for your
escape
again, wiggle your
leg

for you as if I was
your
quantum entanglement
proof
that we have not succumbed
what-
ever that means for
both
of us in this world

Sure

I can appreciate
your not wanting to
die because of me
or struggling with me

this has been careful
campaign, hunger for
eloquence especially
where desire's continuous

through four walls of
concrete a prisoner
of a morsel of space's
demand of tap-root

what am I doing here
who does not mind
your cage as we talk
in letters as if we are

together in penalty of
frightening possibilities
penalty of projection
gobs of vestal words

stare back hoping for
new animations
wanting more than
repair and prosper

so when do we start
scraping shadows of
you from cave walls
into sulfurous buckets

diemethylsulfide heaven
as we all were before
shoved onto desiccating
sand burgeoning sunlight

Fend for yourself

There's no outrunning
an
induced storm when
she's
racing under your
boat
quietly, secretly where
every
seventh wave builds

seems I keep forgetting
this
growth while focusing
on
an unseen shoreline yet
the stern
keeps track for me
and
I can do nothing but

dream
flatness of a sea-born
time
where salty, limpid
people
no longer content
finding
sustenance prey for the
surge

you hear the ghost-bumps
propel
at the back of the boat
begin
to calculate time and
distance
to the zero of home
port
and dry rubber-boots

Perhaps

this waiting is
too
much to explore

weary
wings slowing things
again

how strange when
one
feels familiar strange

shiver
in brute reflex un-
aware

of peace undisturbed
pay
attention to small

move-
ments guiding moment
being

supported by a floral
field
far beyond that

gasp
where noon easily lulled
but

flying again through
grey
twilight seeking a

home
unknown until
reached

Benevolence

Sheared memories all
come
back restless waves
I
would be away I should
away

last evening Thunder
joined
vagus nerve Lightening
simultaneously
got my gut stayed
unafraid

in the smokey light
while
everyone prayed for
showers
relief for dry flowers

who did not remember
we
were safe on a lake
moraine
not the usual chunk of
granite

Found

The cause of ones
death
leaf upon water
matters little now
especially
being delisted from
hospital
line one must pretend
the curl
in the leaf something
like
dying played out in
stream
force until the fall
line
is memorized and on
borrowed
time asking nothing
caught
bobbing in a lee-ward
till
stream rises and the moons
have
gone missing well
beyond
shrieking bird-call
past
so many reflections of
dead
stars with Vega as my
witness

Leela

Gram always said
it
is a cold, ESLanguage
trickle
full of history, separations
that
ebbs from a glacier
frozen
in silent time vertically
but
lumbering through the
lineal
resistance of a yard
sale
picking, choosing to
slowly
evanesce holding
hands
with all terminal
moraines
so soon voiceless

    ii

summer pain flashes
stalks
of tall corn that out-
grew
the woman planter
losing
teeth while waiting
if

drops of silk-oil
will
silence borers who
came
in the darkness un-
announced
as men who spill
words
onto rocks without
terminal
thoughts digesting
so
soon voiceless

    iii

I now see what I meant
paintings
are more than ambiguous
words
as I wait hearing color
of this
icy water,wet rocks knowing
I want
to put my hand in that
water
to turn up the volume in
desire
of eloquence where silent
flowers
turn daggers at gardener's
penalty
of projecting oneself
larger

than a galaxy without under-
going such pain again

Balance

perhaps this is
how
we began as the
result
of external circumstance
unbiased
thinking we are better
than
average with personal
qualities

perhaps this is how
standing
looking straight upwards
as
a vanquished animal
looking
in the remarkable
stillness
of the night-sky for
mid-

night meteors where I
feel
a certain unbalance
unlike
looking down a cliff
but
a straining of Achilles
not
certain of falling forward
or backward

Words
lively, knowing, deep and loving

sun arrived at dead low
tide
sediment at sky's bottom
not
yet embedded in earth's
crust

nothing answered nothing
stones
of our combing language
resting
among alien grains of silica
sand

how many do I have to
recover
before I can understand
tidal
difference between water
washed

or wind blown: which
goes
where in those sentences
discovered
mid phrase and can not trust
completely

Head Tide

where
mackerel and their
tired
eyes meet then
turn
away as the night
goes
silent in this salty
sanity
of low, slow ocean-
water
Trishula, pineal sight,
watch
flooding reflections
jockey
for position in turning
tidal
race toward brackish
color
that allows salt to
dissolve
fish to rest their
aspiration
before moving on

Gravity wins

as silence flings itself
over
Gamma Ray bursts
over
termites flying above
cooling
lady-bugs over our
rheumy
glare of hatred yet
who
wants to be left out
of
our untold story of
ones
own life's invented
character
that we are oh yes
invented
for inclusion's sake
far
from memories
shambles
but proof that we have
evolved
from mere lizard
brain
where everyday is Tabla
Rasa
born into newness of
some
one else s making

while
sequential self understanding
remaining
the same age inside and
that
"the other day " refers to
time
between yesterday and
15
years ago I think

Sic transit

turned heavenward
today
but as usual high,
thin
clouds hid the eclipse
yet
as I left the dock
from
less than two minutes
disruption
of sun's partial no
show
wondering how all
my
ancestry, gloria mundi,
idolized
these especially as my
shadow
ran down my side slightly
red
and ghost-like trailing
into
the white bite heat of
ultra-
violet reflected light
that
I could not stare at
long
as I continued climbing
stairs
toward land yanking
shadow
still red onto coolness

of land
as it was still snapping
at
me writhing snake-like,
hissing

Zhu Xi's reading

In the Analects, his definition of goodness starts with the "golden rule," but he takes his concept further, famously stating that to be good one must be "resolute and firm, simple and slow in speech

> I did not think
> that
> there was so much
> to
> it, this idea of simple,
> slow
> speech as words always
> whirred
> in me as though com-
> pensation
> for ancestors who had
> plenty
> to say but no syntax

>   ii

> simple and slow
> when
> your speech
> from
> oceans to you
> flows
> onto that white-
> ness,
> maybe sand, is
> merely
> adorning ones self
> on

the outside in
effort
to please others and
is
only a smattering of
ancient
desires, sticks and
stones
tearful across hands
left
by the secret swell
of
ancient tidal sweep
left
after timid night's
latent
stillborn shadows

I remain bearish

the Koala Bear in
me
keeps nibbling eucalyptus
leaves
that are protecting your
heart

Inundated

heavenly and colorful,
inflected latinate nouns,
leaves fall in front
of a ricocheting wind

dated, brief shelf life
thinking returns to
horizontal sounds of
historically quiet wishes
I should have acted on

now all that remains
to do is rake slosh-piles
for my son and daughter
re-spreading our cushion
into uncaring joy

how clean the grasp
on the rake's handle
I now lean on, now
how silent my life
has been with them

This room

sit here awhile he
said
at the beginning of
fall
sit here and bear with
me
for I am old and friends
have
gone to the blank of
which
there is no return
as
someone once said
we
go to that other di-
mension
where our souls are
steeped
and drunk in life extension
by
beings we would not
recognize
That was last year and
he
has departed leaving
bones
wherever his daughter
chose
now this room where I
find
fall is upon me, is upon

me
still rent free in this little
room
where everything seems
different

Sunrise, sunset

Panic
what if I never
recognize
anything

unrecoverable streams
unlike
hurricanes, forest fires
fear

there are times
preceding
languages imagined in
deepest

sleep that I hear a
bibelot
that remains softened
breath

held and considered
one
experience's expectation
status

then heard again: every-
one
talking at the same
time

worldwide and turned to
hum
circling our earth
protected

by quickening egocentrics,
water
gushing home to sea,
yet

they can be anguish
prompting
a base of hurry, hurry
hurrying

Add-Ons

By my faith

all sit in darkness
in
this exaggerate
room
of self, a faithful
space:
small, dark room
where
everything or nothing
fits
but seems more or less
real
as a vision of power
that
is unseen by humans
like
broken instruments and
with
our microbial single-
celled
collection joins our
fleet
presence in this smallish
room

Home

On looking at a photo
where
no one would recognize
me
as if an insertion of Glial
stem
this picture trembles twi-
light:
the time when I knew
enough
to head for home on the
Lazy-
Susan of day spinning un-
noticed
in different frames from
beyond
still crying softly to my
self
that this can only be stopped
as
a picture of the past me un-
recognizable

Sanctuary

the trauma room is dark
sinuous
fish with an English prof's
bulbous
eyes have silently entered
nor
there is no one to chase them
out
or back to this morning's
white
fog bow of water droplets
perhaps
driving fish to extremes
seeking
same answers where most
of
us eventually end up with
presumed
50-50 chances eyes closed
feeling
the largest tide of our universe

Imagine

saudade nostalgia for
your
sorrow on a waning
moon

yes
haggard is a good
word
for me now as all
my

rivers hydraulic hunger
have
confluenced fording is
out
of the question while

I
rise and plow due
south
making land by tear-
ing

land while still wishing
for
a reverse to back up
flood
past my spring cooling

those
fires that mock my
water's
bullheadedness
slipping

bank-high further away
swallow
everything in my way
trouble
to steer-clear

haggard
or not to play with my
delta
confluencing in heavy
salt

finding myself settling
down
past startled fish on the
way
to a silent bottom

Another day recuperating:
Emily Dickenson: loneliness = the fear of not being surveyed is a quiet devastation

I am frightened in
another
pre-Dawn wakening
knowing
that soon the sun will
startle
the day, me, into another
day
and what will my diminished
body
tell me; will I rue this day,
my
government shooting its
citizens,
blasting them out of
buildings,
dropping its bombs on hostages
already
being held by our enemies
Is
this our reality of what
extra
terrestrials wanted
leaving
us alone so long ago
to
our own induced famines,
dirty
wars and their eventual
demise
of their own government to

wallow
elsewhere for power
also,
will there be another to do
list
that I basically ignore
under
the guise of these anonymous
words
really meaning something or
other
than to my sensibility and if
so
who in the hell am I today

Ginger

that's your fire-
fanged
mother, charcoal, who
gropes
another now as long as
he
doesn't lie on father's picture
lying

there
where no scrap-book pictures
of
you through out night's
still
heat while I attempted to find
peace
alone in another burning
room

that is darker than any
flame
you've slept through and
hated
by me with her clenching a
picture
of a long dead father's
eyes
staring softly ahead

seeing
neither of us in this dark
mind
that blinks when your stare

Take the A

 step out of your uber
follow
the string of bubbles
we
all need inclusion
what
matters if we end
at
another station where
breasting,
right or left, a similar
land-
scape where maybe we
were
meant: voices arcing
upward
bubbles in confined street
air
disappearing over the
edge
of what is supposed to
happen
boo de ahh dah hurry
and
follow your bubbles

Beaver Moon

spooky, dampness wind-
blown
I always stumble forward,
sommer-
sault inside myself

wanted to tell you
how
great, gray granite stones
lie

quiet, fossil jaw teeth
embedded
in this morning's white
fog

making new friends come
as
bunches of sun-dried
crackling

leaves talked down I
know
what time of the year
I

have lived greenly
through
yet when I proffer to
shake

hands with all my new
friends
they, part wind, laugh
roll
by my open window

as though I were a
god
who means to destroy
them

with a simple rake and
so
bump each other, rolling
towards

the woods that surround
me
on pleasant days, now
winking

at me, capturing my friends
about
their toes with an overall
attitude

of sly-root entitlement
given
by something similar to
mine

On the line

idle hands like flowers fly
through
my night faking sleep, tune-
less,
still clothed as if on a line
break
with a pillow and comforter
hunting
elusive infinite predator
slumber

no one ever threw gran-
ades
but I have been hit by many
unripe
blueberries: thankfully
time
of death replenishes
victims
whose lack of understanding
allows

the rose to wilt and the way
she
went to bed counting little
blue
berries constantly moving
away
from her reach with Poe's
impa
of the perverse smile on

bene-
ficiaries of chance that
can
be so kind to a follower
of
multiple hues belted on
such
a slow moving freezing
conveyor

Night voyage

how to be you in moon
light
try as I may, but for
sure
every night this shiny
dream
the voyage and I are
one,
course, there's always
you
swimming alongside the
boat:
goggles, Orca whites and
blacks
flashing even nightly so
sleep's
impossible then those
joint
aches, tendons etc
I have
to get up head for the bath-
room
eyes open so as not to step
on
cats lying deck-bound in
peaceful
slumber Slumber, I
apostrophise
get up off the the deck
bang
against my head and
let

the cats prowl for a welcome
change
or I'll jump into this GD
water
swipe those goggles, let
salt
crystals pool and sting your
eyes
cause I know you are resting
sleeping

Flume

I keep telling you over and
over
why I choose to live in
sliding
shades of cloudy grayness
during
this life filling those ghosts
brave
enough to reside within

I am
wind borne, drifting on this
wooden
chair, quieter now, that
keeps
me buoyant past rapids
I
would have chosen when
young

in spite of air-less drenchings
or
hidden rocks course alterings

Fear not

when the sky which
is
really the bottom bottom
of
many segments
grows
grim and then to dark-
ness
enveloping me would
like
me to play and laugh
so
that friends are mostly
unaware
now except for my
laughter
that springs from
within
and has not had a
chance
to go dark the way
my
thoughts succumb

I
am unaware she's
watching
her hands disappear as
fear
so she laughs when I
do

setting off our own
horizontal
chain of lightening
between
us and the rest of the
night
is ours with our melan-
choly
language as one of the
hooks
we please her with
close
your eyes I laugh and
we
are safe again open
them
and soon the muskets go
off

Time slot

haunted
whole frame has gone
limp
Umdunbara's white
petals,
long forgotten, stand in
dry
air on rock hard earth
almost
illegal craved legacy

careful not to step Inclinations

it
was comfortably dark
when
I first slow-stopped
there
was nothing and then
sound
dreamily strutted its
self
selfishly contradicting
both
the wind's going's and
coming's

I stare out again
late
without knowing why
shivers
drum below naked

flesh
bumping into my soul
buried
within follicles sway

windless till I meet
my
parents floating a wave
hello
who are not
saying
anything about noise
this
time either and it
stops
as quickly as it
began

on
this floral trust that
begins
our new era- scuse me
did
not know I would fare
this
far final weariness
silenced

Inclinations

it
was comfortably dark
when
I first slow-stopped
there
was nothing and then
sound
dreamaily strutted its
self
selfishly contradicting
both
the wind's going's and
coming's

I stare out again
late
without knowing why
shivers
drum below naked
flesh
bumping into my soul
buried
within follicles sway

windless till I meet
my
parents floating a wave
hello
who are not
saying
anything about noise
this
time either and it

stops
as quickly as it
began
Early December

there is no dissent
sent
from the snow as a
gentle
wind blows it free
of
branches looking for
silent
lees to settle at the
whims
of sculpting wind

how unlike myself
casting
words to show how
busy
my year has been
with-
out the impetuosity
marble
can show before it too
settles
shining for all to

know
how much was left
behind: grit piles and
piles
waist deep like fallen
snow

Early December

there is no dissent
sent
from the snow as a
gentle
wind blows it free
of
branches looking for
silent
lees to settle at the
whims
of sculpting wind

how unlike myself
casting
words to show how
busy
my year has been
with-
out the impetuosity
marble
can show before it too
settles
shining for all to

know
how much was left
behind: grit piles and
piles
waist deep like fallen
snow

To you kind sir

I
a thought more like
an
unexpected handshake
rescued
from crass oblivion

I am not blind yet
can
not see you in my
private
mind, will never know
your
reaction but certain
that
you will read me
word
by word especially
thrilled Hypnagogia

loaded
a branch fetched
down
to rest on shed roof

I used to levitate
with
this tree branch and
have

to remind myself
we
are locked down
with

deep states grasp
also,
this is the warm
wind

that samuraized our
tomatoes
caged to help them
grow

also the same wind
that
frustrated insects and
now

cues ice balls rattling
over
drifts of hard snow
hiding

in pockets waiting
game
over and first spring
smells

sitting beside hoping
they
will teach us when to
open
Hypnagogia

loaded
a branch fetched
down
to rest on shed roof

I used to levitate
with
this tree branch and
have

to remind myself
we
are locked down
with

deep states grasp
also,
this is the warm
wind

that samuraized our
tomatoes
caged to help them
grow

also the same wind
that
frustrated insects and
now

cues ice balls rattling
over
drifts of hard snow
hiding

in pockets waiting
game
over and first spring
smells

sitting beside hoping
they
will teach us when to
open

to hear my name spoken
so
long in future's past un-
expected
but icy clear

Hypnagogia

loaded
a branch fetched
down
to rest on shed roof

I used to levitate
with
this tree branch and
have

to remind myself
we
are locked down
with

deep states grasp
also,
this is the warm
wind

that samuraized our
tomatoes
caged to help them
grow

also the same wind
that
frustrated insects and
now

cues ice balls rattling
over
drifts of hard snow
hiding

in pockets waiting
game
over and first spring
smells

sitting beside hoping
they
will teach us when to
open

Solar stone

crystal-shine falls one-
rousley
into my chest cavity

I've got to keep moving
whiskey
in hand on the watch

for snow as it is now
winter
the temperature slows

any joy in walking
with
older, slipping friends

on once fertile fields
the man
in me, Coleridge today,

feeling like these trees
that
gone deep into my past

posing En-Garde epee
branches
pointing, thinking about

asking for more and
more
of the white expanse

while I strain for
strong
flashes as bright to

trace onto what I
know
will soon be another

branch of memory
soon
green, soon fallen

ah

you now pity
me
like my soul
resting
on its pile of
bones
230 joints un-
willing
to move, wavering
in
their decrepitude
hoping
not to spark pains
quiet
slumber or loosening
souls
grip of thoughts
I
can't do without
while
you watch granite
beneath
me crumble in
acidic
throes and give
no
thoughts or pity
as
you do to me

New Year's Day

hued yellow thoughts
for
toasting again today's
new

nuthatches and woodpeckers
search
my trees sluggish larva
fleeing

frozen heart-wood in-
hospital-
ity during a cold snap
that

has us all bothered and
yet
those reptilian brains
breathing

fire in a surfeit of
icy
food walk, fly by
each

other as though only
they
have the cobbled tree to
them

selves rejoicing, praying
that
this day will last for-
ever

www.ingramcontent.com/pod-product-compliance
Lightning Source LLC
Chambersburg PA
CBHW022109090426
42743CB00008B/780